Islands of Wonder

KAUA'I

Text by Chris & Evelyn Cook

Photography by Douglas Peebles

Mutual Publishing

Library of Congress Control Number: 2011936094
ISBN-10: 1-56647-960-6
ISBN-13: 978-1-56647-960-8

First Printing, June 2012
Second Printing, May 2014
Design by Courtney Young

Mutual Publishing, LLC
1215 Center Street, Suite 210
Honolulu, Hawai'i 96816
Ph: 808-732-1709 / Fax: 808-734-4094
email: info@mutualpublishing.com
www.mutualpublishing.com
Printed in China

INTRODUCTION

Spectacularly scenic Kaua'i is reminiscent of the romantic South Pacific island homelands of its Polynesian settlers who ventured north from the Marquesas and Tahiti a millennium ago. For a photographer, the island's ultra-clear air and startlingly-pure light brings out nature's true hues and endows them with a gem-like quality, from aquamarine lagoons to golden beaches and sapphire seas to emerald mountains. The photographer's palette is further enhanced by rich red volcanic earth and pure white cumulus clouds rolling across azure skies graced with rainbows and the vibrant colors of sunrise and sunset.

Photographer Douglas Peebles accurately records this beauty, and more. His images capture moments when sunlight and moonlight, cloud and mist, reveal the island's innermost soul. On visits spread over decades, Doug has roamed Kaua'i—camera in hand—by land, sea and air, hiking along precarious cliffs, bouncing over waves, and perched in helicopters sans doors, delighting both first-time visitors and longtime kama'āina with his authentic vision of the island.

This portfolio of Douglas Peebles' fine photographic art provides a complete tour of Kaua'i, including the well-watered, windward side from Lihu'e, Wailua and Kapa'a north to Princeville, Hanalei, Hā'ena, and Nā Pali, as well as the drier, leeward side from southernmost Po'ipū to historic Waimea and adjoining towns on the west side that were once the heart of the island's former sugar-based economy.

A side-trip along the rim of Waimea Canyon in the highlands of Kōke'e ends at the trail to the Alaka'i swamp and includes views of the extinct volcano, Mt. Wai'ale'ale, one of the wettest spots on earth and the mountaintop center of Kaua'i.

Aloha, and welcome to the extraordinarily beautiful Garden Island of Kaua'i as seen by one of Hawai'i's most keen-eyed and gifted photographers.

Left: Located between Hanalei and Hā'ena, isolated, lovely Lumaha'i Beach is one of Kaua'i's most photographed features, made famous by the 1958 film, South Pacific. **Previous page:** Ke'ē Beach on Kaua'i's north shore marks the end of the road and the beginning of Nā Pali.
On the cover: Kalapaki Bay, located in Lihu'e near the airport, is one of the first sights seen from the air as arriving flights land.

LĪHU'E TO HĀ'ENA

L ihu'e ("cold chill" in Hawaiian), was given its name in the 1830s by a chieftain named Kaikió'ewa who borrowed it from a cooler clime located in the mountains of O'ahu. With a population around 6,000, Lihu'e is the island's second largest city after the Kapa'a-Wailua area with 10,000. During the height of tourist season, it can take over 30 minutes to drive the seven miles between the two towns, due to heavy traffic. Kaua'i runs on "Hawaiian time," a slower, more leisurely pace retained from a bygone era. So relax, take a deep breath, wave to the other cars stuck in gridlock, and be patient. After passing through Kapa'a and Wailua on the way north to Hā'ena, the traffic thins, the scenery turns rural, there are plenty of beaches and palm trees, and no more stoplights. Hanalei, the heart of the north shore, is about an hour away. Four miles beyond is Hā'ena.

Big, fast waves that break below the cliffs at Kalihiwai Beach on Kaua'i's north shore attract expert surfers. Smaller waves near the middle of the beach draw boogie boarders and kids of all ages.

Above: Outrigger canoe racing has been a popular sport from ancient times to the present. Canoes are around 42 feet long, seat six, and weigh about 400 pounds. They are made either of fiberglass or koa wood.

Left: Queen's Bath along Princeville's rocky shore is a tidal pool fit for royalty when the ocean is calm. When waves crash over the rocks, it can be dangerous, especially in winter.

Opposite page: Hanalei Bay—one of the earth's most scenic natural wonders with a two-mile beach surrounded by mountains—is known for world-class surfing, 5-star accommodations, and fabulous sunsets. The sand-bottom bay is safe for swimming. Snorkeling is best around Princeville.

Above: A popular spot for camping, Hāena Beach Park is a grassy area bordering sand and sea. The view is gorgeous, but the beach is often windy and the water too rough for swimming.

Right: Serene beaches and glorious sunrises are just a short stroll away from the bustle of historic Kapa'a town's restaurants, shops, and galleries on the island's east side.

Opposite page: This little waterfall along Kalihiwai Stream is one of hundreds to be found on Kaua'i. Several of the largest and most spectacular are easily accessible. Others require a long, steep hike, or an arduous trudge through mud and jungle.

Hanalei Bay's two-mile-long, crescent-shaped golden beach is surrounded by a dramatic backdrop of steep mountains laced with waterfalls and wreathed in mist. It wraps around a deep, clear bay of shimmering turquoise, offering swimming, surfing, sailing and breathtaking vistas.

Left: This sunbathing Hawaiian Monk seal is one of dozens that regularly haul-out on local beaches.

Below: The sky catches fire, the ocean turns to flame, and beachgoers watch for the "green flash" as the sun slips below the Hanalei horizon.

Opposite page: Fronds rustle atop coconut palms, surf murmurs soothingly on sand, warm sunlight melts away stress, and fresh ocean breezes carry the scent of plumeria—these are the sensations of an afternoon spent drowsing in a hammock on the beach at Princeville.

Above: An historic lighthouse, a terrific view, and a sanctuary for thousands of wheeling, soaring, chattering seabirds greet visitors to Kilauea Point National Wildlife Refuge on the north shore.

Right: Lydgate State Park, on the east side in Wailua, offers a great beach for sunrise strolls, and a protected sea-water pool for youngsters, complete with colorful little tropical fish. A lifeguard is generally on duty.

Opposite page: Historians believe Polynesian sailors landed in Hawai'i around 700 A.D., followed possibly by shipwrecked Spaniards about 900 years later. Englishman Capt. James Cook, who was credited with the Islands' discovery, first visited Kaua'i in 1778. Modern-day sailors continue to discover the island anew.

Left: Flower bedecked dancers provide a window into the past. In ancient times, hula was a sacred ritual performed in private for the gods.

Below: The three mountain peaks standing guard over Hanalei—Hihimanu, Mamalahoa, and Namolokama—are associated with a number of Hawaiian legends. The highest, Namolokama, is about 4,426 feet. Their forested recesses harbor rare plants, birds and insects found nowhere else on earth. The mythical Menehune, said to reside here, may have been the island's first settlers.

Opposite page: To a loud insistent drumbeat, entertainers at a Kaua'i lū'au perform a Polynesian dance garbed in bright costumes.

Left: Hanalei Bay is a place of many moods. Here, in one of its cheeriest, it smiles on an updated version of an ancient Hawaiian sailing canoe.

Below: Constructed in 1892 and rebuilt a hundred years later, Hanalei Pier has endured hurricanes, huge winter waves, and a ramming during filming of *The Wackiest Ship in the Army*.

Opposite page: Wailua beach is a half-mile-long stretch of golden sand and is often battered by big waves and blasted by strong winds. But when the full moon rises, turning the sea to silver, there's no more magical place to be.

Hanalei Bay is highly photogenic from any angle. This shot, was taken from the bluffs in Princeville. The bay provides safe moorage for yachts in summer, and big waves for surfers in winter.

Left: Since 1946, four generations of the local Smith family have been entertaining guests on the two-mile boat trip up the Wailua River to the Fern Grotto.

Below: It takes about a half-hour by boat and a short stroll by foot to reach the famed Fern Grotto. Hawaiian music, dance, and legends enliven the voyage.

Opposite page, top photo: Iconic Wailua Falls, featured in the 1980s *Fantasy Island* TV series, is 80-feet high and a ten-minute drive north from Lihu'e on Highways 56 and 583. **Bottom photo:** An easy, 45-minute paddle up the Wailua River followed by a short hike is rewarded with a refreshing dip in a natural pool under Secret Falls.

Above, top photo: Taro, most commonly consumed as poi, has been a Hawaiian staple for centuries. Hanalei Valley produces over four million pounds of the crop per year. It's still a favorite food in the Islands.

Bottom photo: One of the most popular spots on Kaua'i's north shore for snorkeling, surfing, and SCUBA, Tunnels Beach never gets too crowded because of limited parking. Come early.

Opposite page: Kalapaki Beach stretches between the lush grounds of the Kaua'i Mariott Resort and the sparkling waters of Kalapaki Bay. Next door is Nāwiliwili Harbor, a busy port where tourist cruise ships dock near the barges and container vessels that supply the island's needs.

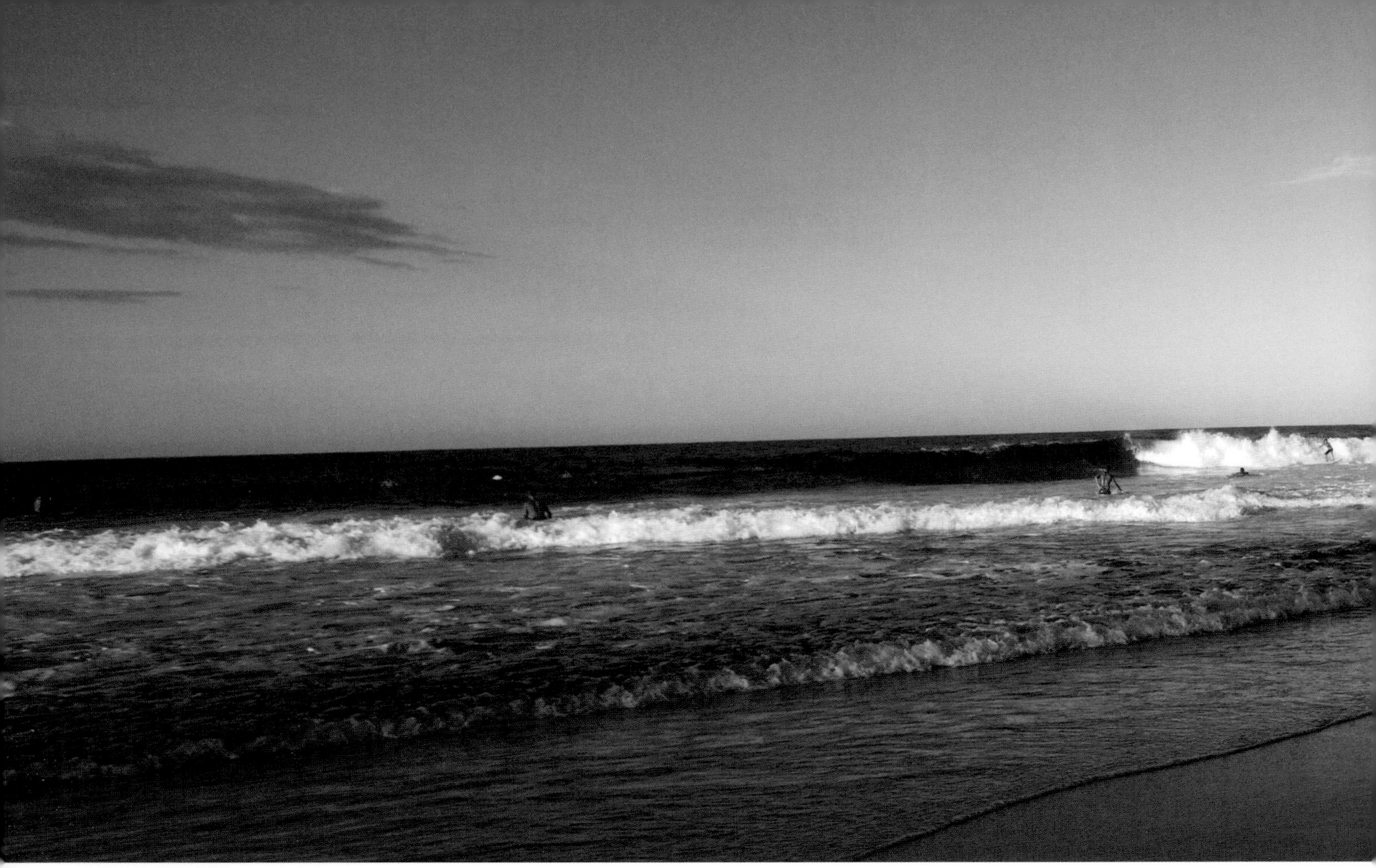

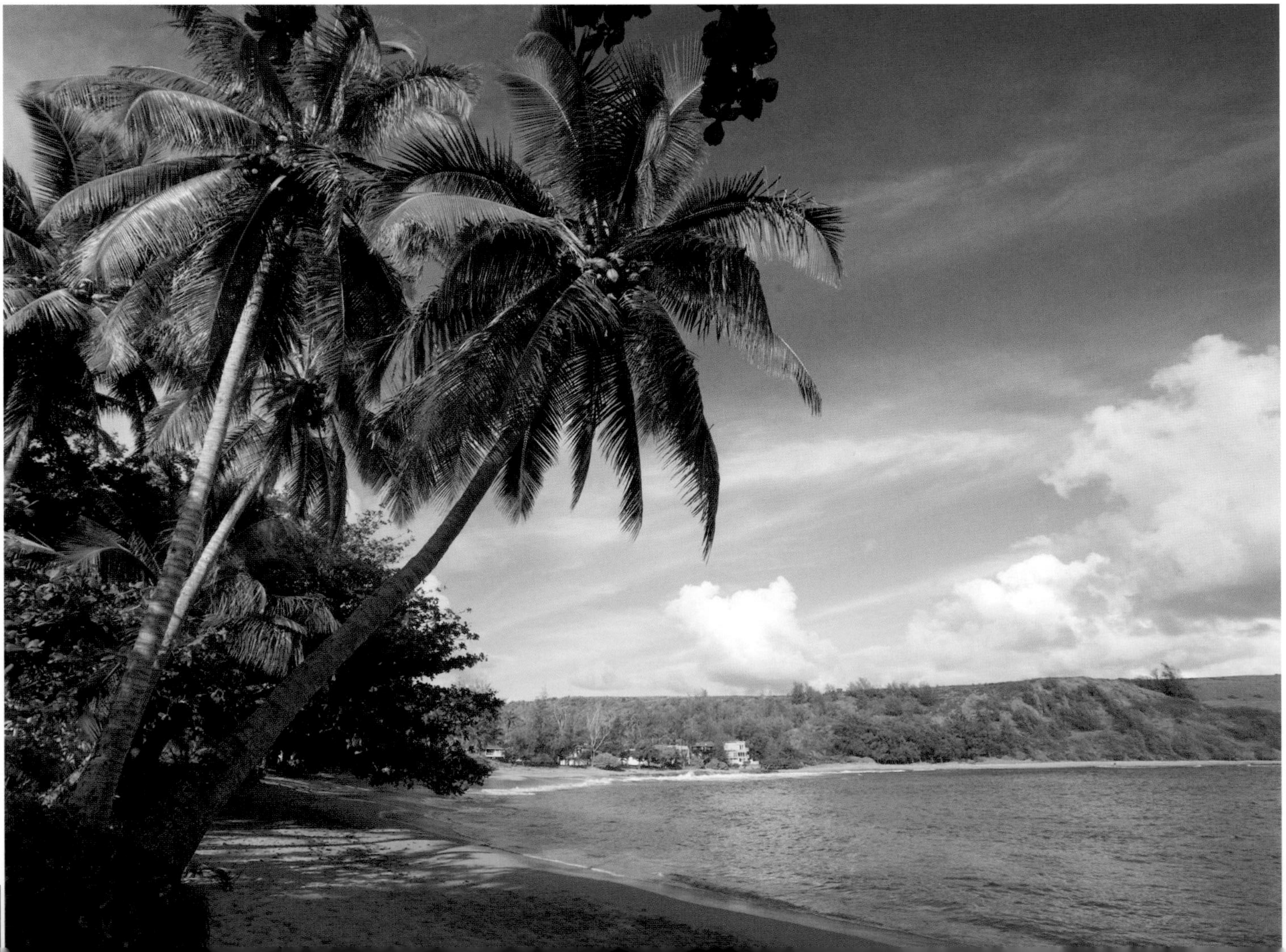

Above: Secret Beach is no secret. But the steep hike and treacherous ocean currents keep the crowds away. The scenery, including views of the Daniel K. Inouye Kilauea Point Lighthouse, is awe-inspiring. Clothing is optional.

Left: The only thing more spectacular than Hanalei's scenery is its surfing. The best waves hit from late fall to spring, and can range up to 30 feet high and higher. Good surf in summer is rare.

Opposite page: Moloa'a, near Kilauea, is one of the island's least-visited beaches. It's small, isolated, and lovely. Swimming can be dangerous and there's no lifeguard, but on calm days the snorkeling is superb.

Above, top photo: Hā'ena is a popular resort area on Kaua'i's north shore with many vacation homes. Long stretches of beach invite leisurely strolls. Strong currents can make swimming difficult. **Bottom photo:** Cowboys—paniolo—have a long history on Kaua'i. Ranches, roundups and rodeos abound.

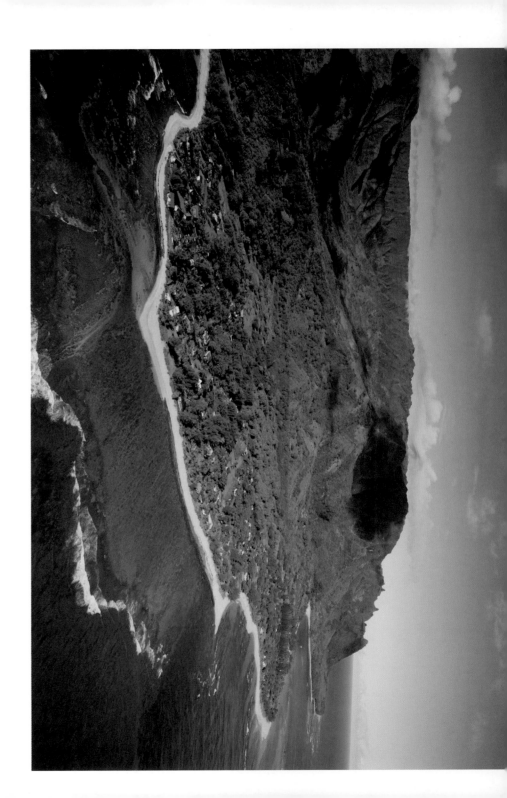

The oceanside pool at the St. Regis Princeville Resort mirrors a Hanalei sunset. After a leisurely catch-of-the-day dinner at the resort's Makana Terrace overlooking the bay, it'll be time for a moonlit meander on the beach. Don't wait up for us!

With its rich volcanic soil, abundant rainfall and 365-days-a-year growing season, Kaua'i produces bumper crops of sugarcane, taro, papaya, banana, mango, coffee, corn, guava, tropical flowers, hardwoods and more. In this view looking south towards Sleeping Giant (Nounou Mountain), the red soil and lush greenery of fertile agricultural lands near Kilauea fill the foreground.

Right: This bird-of-paradise is one of many flowering plants not found on Kaua'i until modern times. Flower lovers have introduced their favorites from around the world. Some have become pests.

Below: Summer in Hanalei brings calm seas and yachts from around the world, as well as thousands of visitors. The beach is so spacious, it never seems crowded.

Opposite page: Rainbows occur frequently on Kaua'i, even when there's no rain. This one has taken advantage of the mist at the foot of Wailua Falls.

Left: Hanalei maintains its rural and friendly farming roots despite having become a major tourist destination and celebrity magnet. Behind the town lies a large network of taro patches.

Below: Kalihiwai Beach, a popular surf spot, is about three miles north of Kilauea town on Kaua'i's north shore.

Opposite page: Limahuli Gardens in Hā'ena, featuring ancient stone terracing and endangered endemic vegetation, is rated the top natural botanical garden in the U.S. for its superior practices in the conservation of water, soil, and rare plants.

Above: Verdant vegetation, golden sand, clear aquamarine water, blue sky, bright sun: this is Larsen's Beach near Moloa'a.

Right: Coconut palms silhouetted against the sunrise at Wailua River State Park stand like royal sentinels guarding the sacred homeland of Kaua'i kings and priests. Ancient temples lie in ruins nearby.

Opposite page: This modern rendition of an ancient tiki, carved by a Kaua'i artist, wears a helmet and a fierce expression. The carving may represent Kū, the Hawaiian war god, worshiped in the past with human sacrifice.

KĒ'Ē BEACH, NĀ PALI, POLIHALE

Kē'ē Beach on Kaua'i's north shore marks the end of the road, and the beginning of Nā Pali ("The Cliffs") a 15-mile stretch of otherworldly spires and pinnacles, lush hanging valleys, sea caves, pristine deserted beaches and sheer precipices that drop 3,000 feet straight down to the ocean. Over the years, the idea has been proposed many times to build a road from Kē'ē through Kōlo'o to the island's west side, following an ancient Hawaiian footpath that snaked along Nā Pali and went up over the mountains and down to Waimea. The cost, however, has always proved prohibitive. There are too many chasms and gulches to span, too many towering mountain walls to tunnel through. For now, the only way to see Nā Pali is by foot, boat, helicopter, or airplane. Polihale Beach lies at the far end of this spectacular series of cliffs, and marks the beginning of Kaua'i's west side.

A tour helicopter takes passengers in for a close look at the extraordinary geological wonder called Nā Pali.

Above: Kalalau, once home to thousands of Hawaiians, is now populated by overnight campers with permits, and a handful of squatters who, entranced by the place, defy the state's orders to leave.

Right: Kayakers enjoy a Nā Pali waterfall. When seas are calm, this is less arduous than hiking into Kalalau. Kayaking has become a popular way for experienced paddlers to explore the area.

Opposite page: Possessing awe-inspiring views of Nā Pali, an ancient heiau (temple) and a shrine to Laka, goddess of the hula—Kēē Beach is a special place. It's also the jumping off spot for the 11-mile trail that ends in Kalalau Valley.

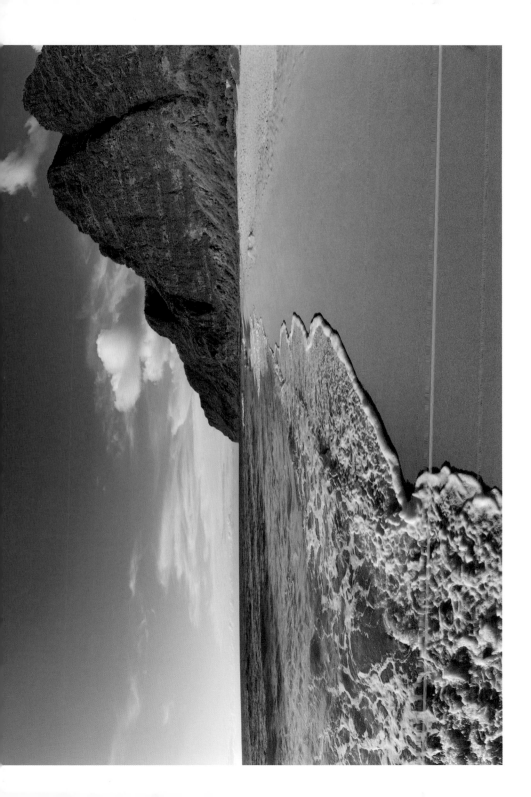

Above: Where Nā Pali ends, Polihale Beach State Park and the west side of Kaua'i begin. Vehicles without four-wheel drive often get stuck in the mud on the primitive dirt road to Polihale and need a tow.

Left: Many hikers choose to explore Nā Pali via the Kalalau Trail, intending to trek the full 11 miles, only to turn back after discovering the path climbs steeply for 1,500 feet, then drops 1,500 feet—over and over again.

Opposite page: Kalalau Beach is beautiful—and dangerous. It's easy to get sucked out by the undertow and hard to get back to shore. Waves slam the sand with great force in summer, and greater force in winter. Currents are fierce even when the ocean looks calm. Too many swimmers have drowned here.

Above: Kēʻē Beach is one of those places where visitors suddenly stop, gaze around in wide-eyed wonder, sigh, and say to themselves, "Ah, the real Hawaiʻi." (It happens a lot on Kauaʻi.)

Right: Small tour boats provide front-row seats for viewing Nā Pali. They're skippered by knowledgeable guides who can read the local waters and conditions. Friendly dolphins often tag along.

Opposite page: This is just one of the many splendid sights that greet visitors to Kalalau. Ancient stone terraces back in the valley are the only visible remnants of Hawaiians who lived here until the early 1900s.

Following page: Those who return to Kauaʻi year after year often speak in superlatives about Kēʻē as their favorite beach: "Unbelievably clear water" ... "Swimming there was like being in a dream or movie." ... "Too beautiful to be real." ... "Felt like I was in another world, or on a different planet." ... "Exotic and sensual." ... "Something sets it above all the other beaches on Kauaʻi."

Left: Polihale Beach is a great place to view Nā Pali's grandeur. Head west on Highway 50 from Waimea to the end of the paved road. Continue straight over the rough, dirt road until you're there. If you don't have four-wheel drive, you might get stuck.

Below: Nā Pali garbed in sunset splendor, as seen from Kē'ē Beach.

Opposite page: A kayak trip from Kē'ē to Polihale along Nā Pali is an adventure that will never be forgotten. Local outfitters provide gear and supplies but warn that paddling this isolated coastline is not for beginners. Weather and sea conditions may change suddenly and radically, and often there's no one around to help in a rescue.

LĪHU'E TO WAIMEA CANYON

Upon landing at the Līhu'e Airport, first-time visitors will sometimes ask a friendly local about the island's best places—the most special that aren't to be missed. The reply generally goes something like this, "Be sure to see the north shore and Nā Pali. Come back here to Līhu'e to eat awesome noodles at Hamura Saimin, then head to the west side. Go snorkeling at Po'ipū—the fish will swarm around you if you feed them frozen peas—and by the time you get to Waimea you'll be hungry again, so try some manapua or bento, or stop by Ishihara Market for the best sushi ever. Then go see Waimea Canyon. Drive up the mountain to Kōke'e—it's nice and cool up there, 3,500 feet—and hike the canyon rim. You won't believe the views. Or start walking right there in Waimea and hike to the top from the bottom, except you've got to be in really good shape for that. Here, try some of this spam musubi. It's 'ono."

The first sight seen by many as the airliner approaches Kaua'i: Kipū Kai, a series of small, sandy coves tucked against the rugged Hā'upu Mountains. The easiest way to get there is by boat.

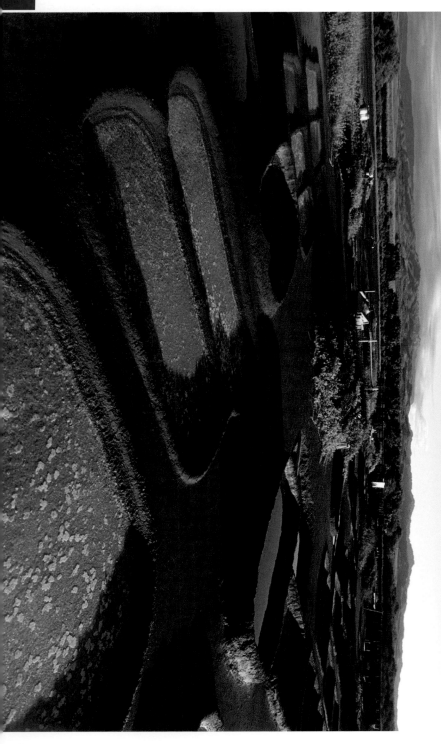

This page: Coconut palms and verdant mountains—clear, blue-green waters and sparkling sands: Kalapaki is the finest beach in the Lihu'e area and a favorite playground for both visitors and locals.

Opposite page, top photo: Shrouded in clouds much of the time, Mt. Wai'ale'ale, at 5,148 feet, is one of the world's wettest spots, averaging 450 inches of annual rainfall. In 1982, a record 666 inches fell.

Bottom photo: At ancient salt ponds near Hanapēpē, Hawaiians continue to make salt by evaporating sea water as their ancestors did centuries ago. They give the salt away as gifts or in trade, but never sell it.

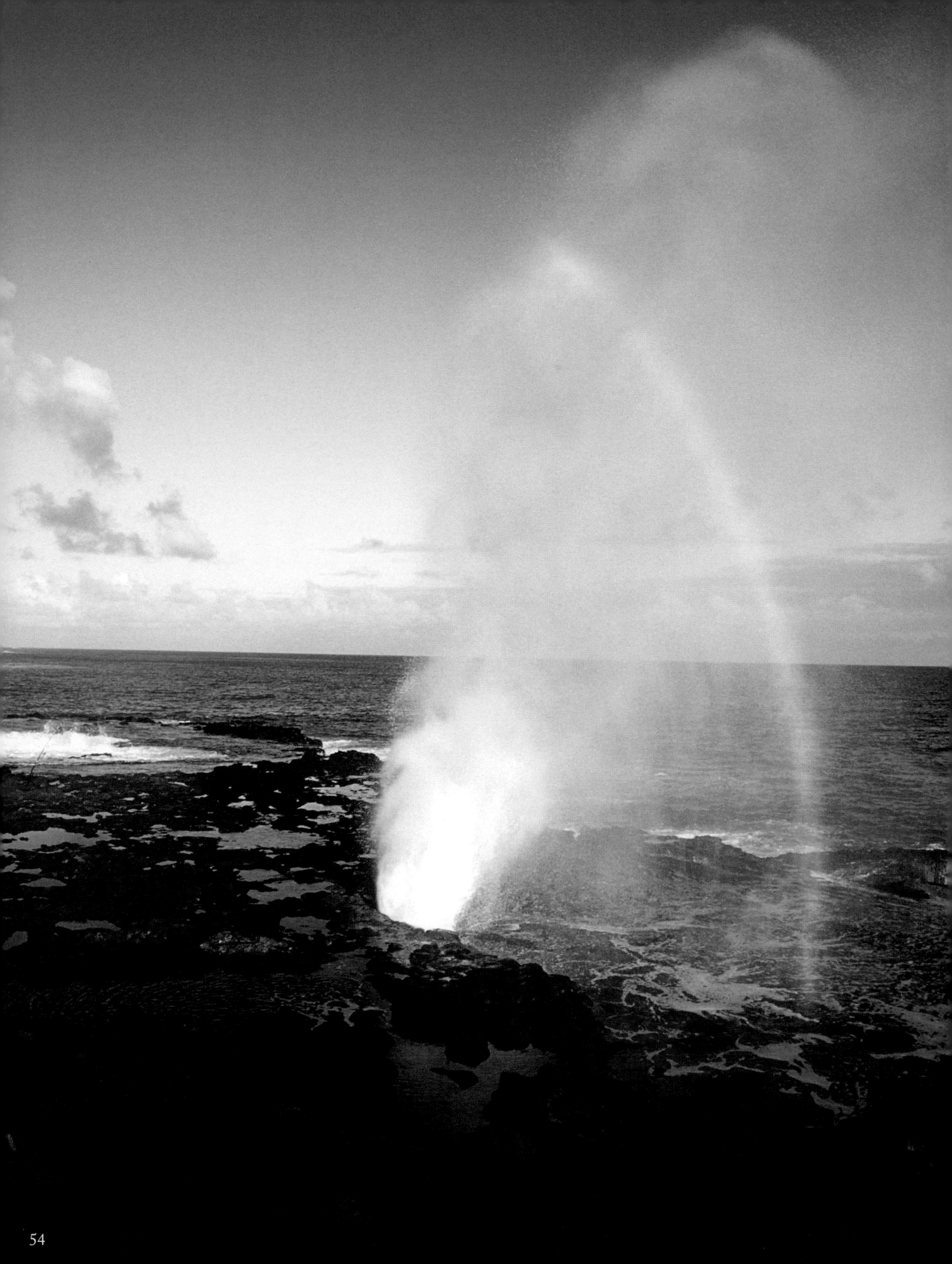

Above: Hawaiians dance in Waimea to honor Kaua'i's favorite son, Kōloa-born Prince Jonah Kūhiō Kalanianaʻole. Prince Kūhiō Day, a state holiday, is celebrated on March 26, the prince's birthday, with parades, music and festivities.

Left: In the misty Alakaʻi Swamp, an elevated trail keeps rare species safe from hiking boots—and feet dry.

Opposite page: Spouting Horn, Poʻipū: the surging ocean fills a hollow lava tube and shoots a geyser into the air like a surfacing whale. The mingling of mist and sunlight results in a rainbow.

Right: Pākalā is a west side beach where the ocean appears a deep chocolate brown due to eroded red soil washed into the water by a nearby river. It's also a favorite surf spot despite frequent sharks.

Below: The long, winding drive up to 3,500-foot Kōke'e State Park offers scenic rewards like this view of Kalalau Valley and the blue Pacific. Even from here, whale spouts can sometimes be spotted.

Opposite page: Lovely Kamapua'a Falls takes its name from a mythical Hawaiian demi-god who was half human and half pig. A lover of the fire-goddess, Pele, he was one of the lucky few the hot-tempered volcano queen didn't dispatch in a flood of molten lava.

Above: This sliver of sand, Makaweli Beach, is one of the few bits of land in the area not owned by the Robinson family. The Robinsons, whose ancestors settled on Ni'ihau and Kaua'i in 1864, own the island of Ni'ihau and much of the west side.

Left: The strip of greenery between the river and Menehune Fish Pond grows atop a 900-foot-long stone wall built sometime before the Polynesians arrived in the islands. No one knows who built it, or when.

Opposite page: Palms sway in the sunset as the last beachgoers gather towels, beach mats, coolers, and kids and load up the car. After a hard day of sun bathing, no one feels like cooking, so what'll it be? 'Ahi bruschetta at the Beach House in Poi'pū? A tender T-bone at Wrangler's in Waimea? Or maybe Crispy Coconut Shrimp at Duke's on Kalapaki Beach? It's a tough life, but someone has to live it.

Left: Using the same method Hawaiians have used for centuries a net fisherman on a Poʻipū reef braves surf and slippery rocks to bring home dinner.

Below: Outrigger sailing canoes race out of Nāwiliwili Harbor, the island's primary commercial port. Port Allen on the west side is also an active harbor providing facilities for Navy boats and other vessels.

Opposite page: A tour helicopter zooms in for a close-up of Manawaiʻopuna Falls on west side lands belonging to the Robinson family, who owns about 45,000 acres on Niʻihau and Kauaʻi. Portions of the 1993 dinosaur flick *Jurassic Park* were filmed here.

This page: This spit of sand goes out to a rocky reef at Poʻipū Beach Park. The sand gets washed away certains times of the year, one can usually walk out. The snorkeling is good on both sides when the water is calm. Along the coast lies the Marriott Waiohai Beach Club.

Opposite page, top photo: Serene, uncrowded Māhāʻulepū is the only accessible undeveloped stretch of coastline on Kauaʻi's south shore.

Bottom photo: A hiker admires Waimea Canyon's vivid colors which seem to change with the light.

Waimea Canyon is ten miles long, a mile wide and more than 3,500-feet deep. Its summits, cliffs and ravines harbor herds of feral goats and wild pigs along with a host of rare native plants, birds and insects that are being extinguished by introduced species and human activities.

64

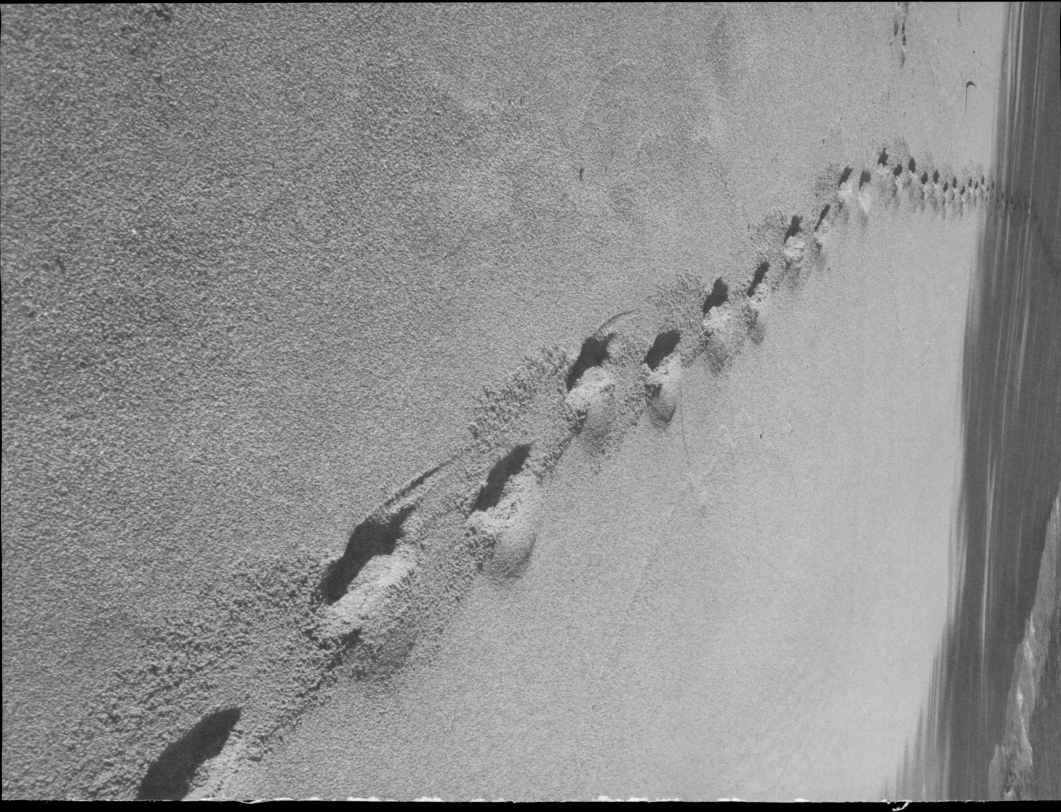